Creatively Speaking:

How to Communicate

Through Art

Written by Jaimee Z. Canty

Greeting Card Artist, Author &
Founder of Jaimee's Hand-Designed Greeting Cards, LLC

<u>With Loving Dedication:</u>

I dedicate this book to my beautiful paternal grandmother, Ethel Pearl Canty and to my lovely maternal grandmother, Lillie Mae Graham.

I also honor the life and legacy of my late paternal great-grandmother,
Eliza Pearl McDonald, best known to her grandchildren as "Gran."

Because I witnessed the grace, class, and style of these ladies, it is easy for me to create beauty where there is none.
I only have to think of them.

Table of Contents

Introduction

Chapter 1:

Speaking in Spirals

Chapter 2:

Talking in Circles

Chapter 3:

Creating a Canvas

The Artwork on the Cover

The black and white spiraling artwork on
the cover is entitled "Rocks & Swirls."

It was handmade by this book's author,
Jaimee Z. Canty, in 2004.

It's also featured on the website
www.jaimeesgreetingcards.com
under the *Miniatures & Artwork* tab.

Introduction

Art is a common, yet sometimes uncommonly wonderful, way for artists to communicate how they think, how they feel, and how they see the outside world.

Artists usually develop their own style, so that their artwork is distinct and has its own signature. I know I create art in such a way that those who have seen it before will recognize my touch should they see my work again.

Even in other art mediums, such as singing, the artist tries to create a unique sound. They want their voice and vocal style to be immediately recognizable.

Most artists realize that you have to be extraordinary, and give the people something that they have not heard or seen before. That is what separates greatness from mediocrity.

For me, art offers an opportunity to speak a message without having to say a word. Often times, I will see a vision in my head of something that I want to make. Then there are other times that I will make a greeting card or an artistic piece without knowing what the end result will be.

Both approaches to creating art are acceptable. Different people simply have different processes and methods they use in order to produce a creative work. Part of the beauty of being an artist and a writer is that I have total freedom to say what I want to say, the way I want to say it.

Even the smallest thing can display a deeper meaning. For instance, I have gone on vacation several times to a large amusement park with my maternal grandmother. So when she graduated (at the wonderful age of 88) from a computer boot camp program, I made a special graduation card.

The card stock's paper was velvet-y royal blue. The card's front featured a little white cloth graduation gown and other decorative accents. I wanted to help her celebrate her latest accomplishment, and I thought it would be fun to put something on the card related to the amusement park.

So, I put a diamond-like accent with the head, face, and ears of the amusement park's main character on the card. Simple additions like that can really make a gift even more special and significant. Art gives you the chance to share those sentimental

www.jaimeesgreetingcards.com

memories of the good old days with the special people in your life.

I was also excited to go to my grandmother's graduation. I applaud a person, especially at that age, who has not given up on life. When I worked as a nursing assistant, I learned that some seniors simply reach a point where they no longer desire to live or participate in life. And that is unfortunate, because an older person is a living library, and they really have so much they can teach us.

Creating art with you own hands and sharing it with others is an act of love. People like to know that someone took time to design something especially with them in mind. It's always best to give people their flowers while they can still smell them, enjoy them, and appreciate them.

Chapter 1:
Speaking in Spirals

My hand-designed artwork "Rocks & Swirls," is featured on the cover of this book. When I made it in 2004, I used tiny, pebble-sized black and white fish tank rocks to create the circular spirals. I used a brush-on, clear coating so that it would have a glossy look once it dried. It took me about five days to complete. Most people would never dream of using fish-tank pebbles to create a canvas-based work of art.

By making art that's distinct, I help people to better understand me. Other artists do this as well. For instance, I am more of an introvert. Unless there is point or a purpose, I don't talk just for the sake of talking. Some people are uncomfortable with silence and will run their mouths about nothing just to fill up quiet space.

Then too, I have known people who will talk and talk and talk, but there really is no message or point to their conversation. After a while, people start to tune out and ignore the super talker. It's best to say less and listen more. Then when you do speak, people are more inclined to give you their full attention.

Speaking of spirals, you can create a winding road of trouble for yourself by ignoring your own reality. It's okay to take an honest look and an honest inventory of your current situation. Plastering that fake smile across your face will not change the fact that you are miserable inside.

If you don't like your life, you have to be willing to put forth the work and the effort to change your life. Unless you are making moves that will open other doors for you (be that by taking online classes for a new degree or by starting and growing your own business), then you will be in the same rut next year that you are in right now.

I have found that some people will say they want to do better and live better, but they really don't. People often say that we should reach out and help one another. Sometimes that is true, but that person has to want the help.

That's why the well-known alcoholic support group has its members to say their name and to admit that they are an alcoholic. Admitting that there is a problem is the first step towards sincere change and improvement. But that desire has to come from that person's heart, and they have to be committed to making those changes.

Otherwise, you are just wasting your time calling yourself helping them. You can control yourself, but you will never be able to change and control another adult. As hard as it may be, you have to accept that that person is not going to think like you, live like you, or do what you would do. You just have to decide if it's worth it to keep that person in your life.

There is also a value in having discernment and realizing when someone is just trying to push your buttons and get you angry. That's a sneaky spiral that you don't want to fall into. People cannot argue with you if you are not arguing back. And then if someone is walking by, you want them to clearly see who the fool is.

For instance, I used to work in a clerical job with extremely high customer contact. I would say 98 percent of the customers would come in, get what they needed, and go home. They didn't cause any problems or disrespect anyone.

Then there was that two percent who would come into the building with a sour expression and a nasty attitude. You could say "good morning," or just a generic "hello" to these individuals, and they would bite your head off. They were mad at the world, and no matter how nice you tried to be, you were never going to satisfy or please them.

People behaving in this manner are really not at peace with themselves. They are usually in a place of not truly loving themselves. I'm not talking about the person who has an occasional bad day or that individual who has just suffered a loss. There are seasons and situations in life where sadness is warranted.

I'm referring to those individuals who are always belligerent, permanently fussing and cussing, and always spewing venom no matter where they go. What people who act like that don't realize is that they could just as easily turn their anger around and use it in a positive way.

Anger is an emotion placed within us for a reason: it's intended to excite us into action. It's negative only if and when you don't know how to use it. For example, there is a growing wave of people who have started holistic health websites and who preach the natural foods gospel.

Most of these health-food gurus will tell you that they grew angry at what they call the "sick care" system. No matter how many medical doctors, or pills, or surgeries they tried, they still found themselves in poor health. So instead of using their anger to destroy medical clinics and hurt people, they opted to use their anger to help themselves and others.

These individuals made a conscious decision to take their health into their own hands, instead of blaming someone else for their illnesses. They have cut the known medical establishment a loose. Sometimes you have to cut people, and places, and things out of your life if you hope to improve your health.

Chapter 2:
Talking in Circles

The circle of creativity is such that an artist can create a work of art that speaks one thing to one person, and something else to the next person. For instance, I took a blank white canvas and used varying shades of soft felt fabric to create the background. I used a combination of dried cinnamon sticks, wooden beads, glass beads, rattan wire, and a large teddy bear sticker.

I painted the sides of the canvas sienna brown. That particular canvas artwork is largely brown, and brown is the dominant color in my home. Brown is associated with stability and purpose, just like the brown wood of a tree.

The artwork, which I named "Teddy Bear Time," can be viewed on my website under the *Miniatures and Artwork* tab. Some people have seen the art piece mentioned and primarily noticed the soft teddy bear in the center.

Others have stated it reminded them of chocolate. A few people thought it looked like a patchwork quilt.

Each response reflected what each individual took away from the art. And that's perfectly fine. It's a good thing to create artwork that people respond to on an emotional level. Then, too, people have a way of seeing what they need to see when they look at art.

It's the same way with life. We may walk into the world under circumstances outside of our control. However, upon reaching adulthood, it is completely up to us to decide who and what we want to become. Some people choose to surround themselves with people who are not encouraging, who are not setting any goals, and who are not excited about life.

It's just like white potatoes cooking in a large pot with other vegetables. The potatoes absorb the flavors of the other foods they are cooking with. People are not that much different. You find yourself taking on the habits, mannerisms, and behaviors of the people you spend your time with.

That can be good or bad. There are times when you have to let go of people (even if those people are biologically related to you) and things that hinder you and hold you back. If that individual brings nothing but chaos and trouble into your life, you should consider cutting them loose.

If you are no better off than when you started, then it might be high time to move on. For instance, if you have not gained anything in the last two years of working that low-paying, energy-draining job, then why not seek out a more fulfilling future?

I know how it feels to have a heavy sense of dread and despair every Sunday. It's because you know Monday means another five-day, patience-trying, misery-filled work week.

It is never wrong to love yourself. It is never wrong to set standards in your life. I have been in situations where I was minding my own business, and an individual would mistake my quietness for weakness.

I had to help them in that area, and educate them (all the while speaking calmly) on Jaimee Z. Canty's standards for social interaction. You have to let people know when you do not like how they treat you or how they talk to you.

But if a particular person or situation is not worth it, let it go. You can't debate every minor issue, nor can you argue every little point. If you develop a reputation for being too fussy and argumentative, you will not be paid any attention when you do have something important to say. So choose your battles carefully and wisely.

I have found that a little bit of fire is needed if you want to let people know you are serious. When I say fire, I am not talking about screaming until you are hoarse, or shouting obscenities, or physically assaulting people. I am talking about being assertive and clearly and firmly letting people know when what they are doing is unacceptable.

Cold preserves and maintains, but nothing stays the same once it has been touched by fire. It is best to have standards for yourself.

www.jaimeesgreetingcards.com

Many stores and websites today offer any product or service you can think of. But there is not a store in the world where you can pick up some dignity or buy some self-respect.

Chapter 3:

Creating a Canvas

Creating a canvas means that a once plain, white canvas is going to tell whatever story that its creator wants to tell. The differences are what make life interesting. Art is a vocation that allows for some flexibility and creativity.

For the most part, there is no good or bad or right or wrong way to produce art. There are times and places where structure and order are a must. On the other hand, I enjoy the freedom of painting, designing, and art-making in my own way.

Even in the writing-based professions, there are rule books and style books that must be adhered to. When I was print journalism major in college, the professors introduced us to the standard writing style book used by major news outlets.

The style and rule book served as a standard bearer for all newspapers across the country. It helped to create word-use consistency among the different news groups. Then each newspaper office would usually have its own in-house style book that always trumped the rules in the national style book.

Publishers would often make these changes according to the communities they served. Each newspaper needed to provide the news, but it also needed to be relevant to its specific audience.

As a former newspaper editor, I understand how important it is to be able to connect with your readers. Otherwise, people will see no need to read your particular newspaper.

www.jaimeesgreetingcards.com

When I was a sophomore in college, I became editor-in-chief of the student newspaper. Students rarely used the paper for its intended purpose. (They would use it cover the table while they ate shrimp and crab legs, for example). So, I knew I needed to make some real changes, real quick to get the students reading the paper again.

I easily identified the paper's main problem: It was little more than a reprinted, regurgitation of the university's press releases. Students do not care about professor so-and-so's latest paper presented at this conference or at that symposium. Public relations and journalism are two different things.

It is the job of the public relations office to relay positive stories about the university president, the administration and staff, and the newly-funded campus buildings. Students want a student newspaper that's educational, a newspaper that's truth-telling, and a newspaper that speaks to their college experience.

So I made it a policy that we would not print anymore press releases. I created a section where we highlighted a student each month. The first person we featured was a single mom, a nontraditional (meaning she was over age 22) college student, and a war veteran. Her story of juggling her work life and her family was powerful on so many levels. I also added a section where we would print twenty rhetorical questions related to the campus, the staff, or the nearby community.

It wasn't long before students would wait with anticipation for the paper to be delivered to the dorms. I took the paper from nothing to something, just by painting its canvas in a different way. When I last looked at the

www.jaimeesgreetingcards.com

university newspaper online, they were still using the style and writing tactics that I came up with back in 1998!

Whether it is through a newspaper article, a paint canvas, a textured artwork, or a book of poetry, an artist can offer a look into the human experience. As you travel through life, you may encounter unexpected curves and unforeseen spirals. But press forward by painting yourself a meaningful and fulfilling life canvas.

Jaimee's Contact Information

Main Website

www.jaimeesgreetingcards.com

Etsy (Order Greeting Cards Online on Etsy)

https://www.etsy.com/shop/JaimeesGreetingCards

Facebook

www.facebook.com/JaimeeCanty

Google Plus

https://plus.google.com/102555406968472898402/posts

Pinterest

www.pinterest.com/jaimeecanty

Twitter

https://twitter.com/JaimeeCanty

Jaimee's Hand-Designed Greeting Cards

Jaimee's Greeting Cards offers you an opportunity to give more than a greeting card…you can gift them with an experience.

With our *NEW Prosperity Gemstone Greeting Cards*, you will gift them with increase. You will gift them with more youthfulness. You will gift them with more possibilities.

You see, natural gemstones work with the body's natural chemistry to encourage physical and mental rejuvenation. A gemstone greeting card will set your gift apart at that next celebration, and just having one in the room will bring positive energy.

www.jaimeesgreetingcards.com

Legal Disclaimer:

Jaimee Z. Canty, Jaimee's Hand-Designed Greeting Cards LLC, nor Jaimee's Greeting Cards intends for any natural gemstone to replace the advice or instruction of your physician. Gemstones are a natural method to *assist with* physical and emotional healing. Do not change your health regimen or stop taking prescriptions unless instructed to do so by your physician.

www.ingramcontent.com/pod-product-compliance
Lightning Source LLC
Chambersburg PA
CBHW051418170526
45165CB00004BA/1877

* 9 7 8 1 5 0 0 9 8 4 5 6 4 *